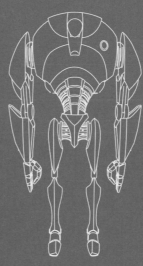

Penguin
Random
House

**Senior Editor** Emma Grange
**Project Editor** Matt Jones
**Project Art Editor** Jess Tapolcai
**Designer** Chris Gould
**Pre-Production Producer** Siu Yin Chan
**Senior Producer** Mary Slater
**Managing Editor** Sarah Harland
**Managing Art Editor** Vicky Short
**Publisher** Julie Ferris
**Art Director** Lisa Lanzarini

**Illustrations by** Jess Tapolcai and Luis Ribeiro

**For Lucasfilm**
**Editor** Caitlin Kennedy
**Creative Director of Publishing** Michael Siglain
**Art Director** Troy Alders
**Story Group** James Waugh, Pablo Hidalgo,
Leland Chee, Matt Martin, and Emily Shkoukani
**Asset Management** Tim Mapp, Nicole
LaCoursiere, Sarah Williams, and
Gabrielle Levenson

First American Edition, 2020
Published in the United States by DK Publishing
1450 Broadway, Suite 801, New York, NY 10018

A catalog record for this book is available from the Library of Congress.
ISBN: 978-1-4654-9006-3

DK books are available at special discounts when purchased in
bulk for sales promotions, premiums, fund-raising, or educational use.
For details, contact: DK Publishing Special Markets,
1450 Broadway, Suite 801, New York, NY 10018
SpecialSales@dk.com

Printed in China

A WORLD OF IDEAS:
SEE ALL THERE IS TO KNOW

www.dk.com
www.starwars.com

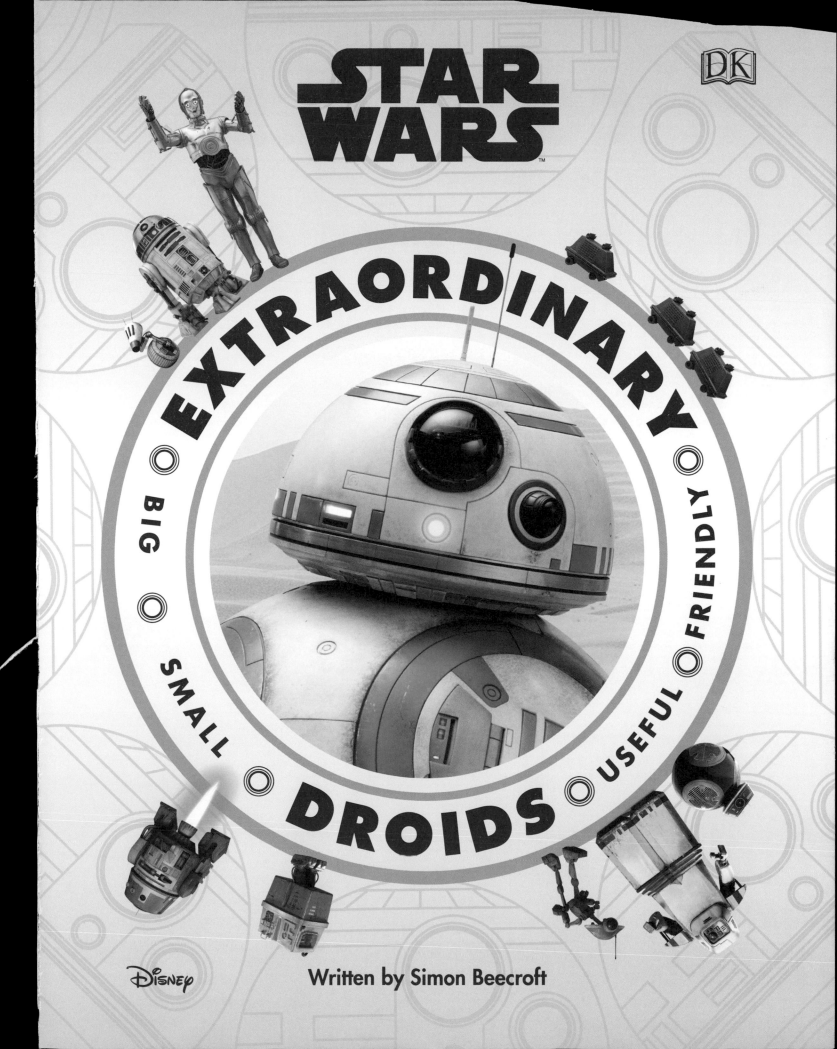

# Star Wars

## EXTRAORDINARY DROIDS

BIG ◎ SMALL ◎ USEFUL ◎ FRIENDLY

Written by Simon Beecroft

Disney

DK

# CONTENTS

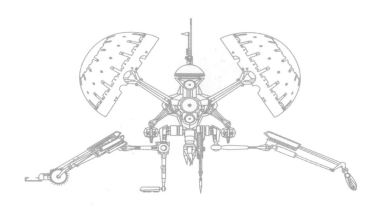

**8**    Introduction

**10**    Buzz Droid

**12**    DRK-1 Probe Droid

**14**    ASN Courier Droid

**16**    Mouse Droid

**18**    D-O

**20**    BB-9E

**22**    CB-23

**24**    BB-8

**26**    LIN-V8K Mining Droid

**28**    PA-LT4

**30**    AZI-3

**32**    Chopper

**34**    GA-97

**36**    WED Treadwell Droid

**38**    R2-D2

**40**    R4-P17

**42**    Bucket

**44**    Gonk Droid

**46**    R5-D4

**48**    Pit Droid

**50**    DJ R3X

**52**    Crab Droid

**54** First Order Sentry Droid

**56** FD3-MN

**58** Imperial Probe Droid

**60** 4-LOM

**62** FX-7 Medical Droid

**64** FLO

**66** Emmie

**68** K-OHN

**70** B-U4D

**72** P4T-GM

**74** AP-5

**76** C-3PO

**78** SE8 Waiter Droid

**80** L3-37

**82** Professor Huyang

**84** Droideka

**86** Police Droid

**88** 2-1B

**90** EV-9D9

**92** Battle Droid

**94** Commando Droid

**96** Super Battle Droid

**98** IG-88

**100** R1-G4

**102** MagnaGuard

**104** Dwarf Spider Droid

**106** Peazy

**108** K-2SO

**110** CC-4M

**112** Vulture Droid

**114** Droid Tri-fighter

**116** Hailfire Droid

**118** Glossary

**120** Height Index

# INTRODUCTION

In the *Star Wars* galaxy, droids are robots who help others. They are found everywhere and do lots of different jobs. Some droids help people fly starships, while others serve food to guests. Droids come in all shapes and sizes. Most droids are helpful and friendly. But some are dangerous! You'll meet all kinds of amazing droids in this book, and learn about all the things they do. They are arranged from smallest to largest. The index pages at the back show them all together in height order. Can you find a droid that is the same size as you? Also, remember to use the glossary at the end of the book. That's where you'll learn what any tricky words mean.

**Are you ready to meet the droids?**
**Then let's go!**

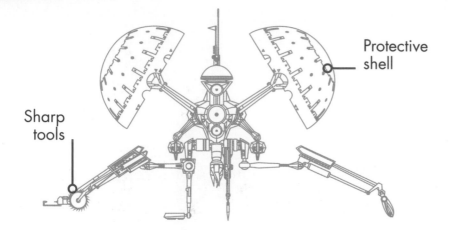

Sharp tools

Protective shell

# BUZZ DROID

Imagine you are flying a starship during a battle. Suddenly, a bunch of little round balls stick to the side of your ship. Watch out! These balls are about to pop open. Inside the round shell of each ball is a buzz droid. Soon, the droid's arms and legs will start to drill, cut, and saw their way through the sides of your ship. Bang! Whir! Buzz! They will try to damage your ship to make it crash or explode! To get rid of them you'll have to knock them off into space.

**A good way to get rid of a buzz droid is to give it an electric shock. Aim for its red photoreceptor eyes!**

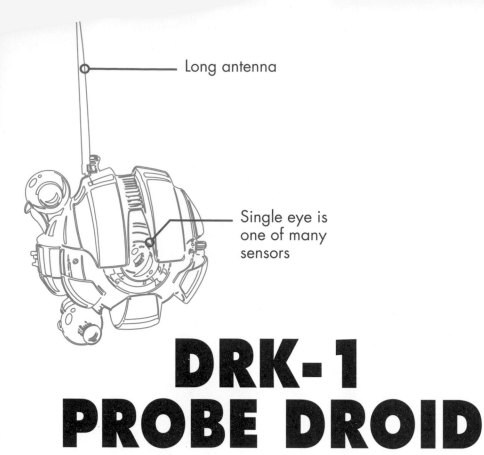

Long antenna

Single eye is one of many sensors

# DRK-1 PROBE DROID

Tiny DRK-1 "dark eye" probe droids are flying spies. Even worse, the galaxy's dark warriors, the Sith, use them to hunt enemies. DRK-1s are controlled by a device worn on the wrist. They sneak around silently listening to conversations. Their size and black body casing means they are hard to spot. The droids, however, have powerful sensors to seek out and spot their prey, even in darkness. When they find their target, they immediately contact their master and wait for further instructions.

**Probe droids sometimes carry weapons to stun or capture their prey. Watch out!**

Shiny exterior is not blaster proof

# ASN COURIER DROID

Keep watch on your windows! This sneaky ASN-121 droid can fly up to the outside of a building, silently make a hole in the window, and slip inside. Courier droids are used to carry information. But ASN droids can carry all kinds of weapons and tools, too, including a harpoon launcher and a spy sensor. Because of this, they have even been used by criminal bounty hunters seeking a way to transport poisonous darts. Nasty!

**If you grabbed hold of an ASN droid, it could lift you into the air. Even Jedi Obi-Wan Kenobi has been carried in this way!**

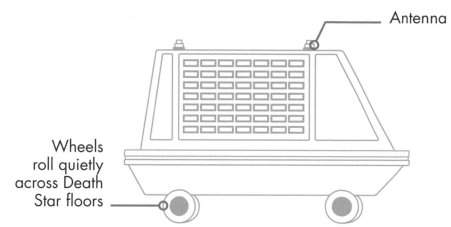

Antenna

Wheels roll quietly across Death Star floors

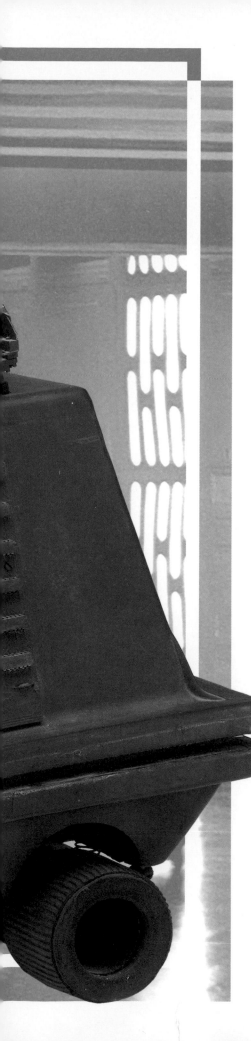

# MOUSE DROID

**D**o you know how big the Death Star is? It is the size of a moon, with endless corridors. That's when you need an MSE-6 droid, also known as a mouse droid. These little droids can show you around. But they can only do one job at once. If they are not escorting guests or prisoners, they are cleaning the floors or doing a repair. Mouse droids can carry secret messages in their roof racks. If captured, they are programmed to self-destruct!

**Big, hairy Wookiee Chewbacca once scared a mouse droid. It squeaked and ran away!**

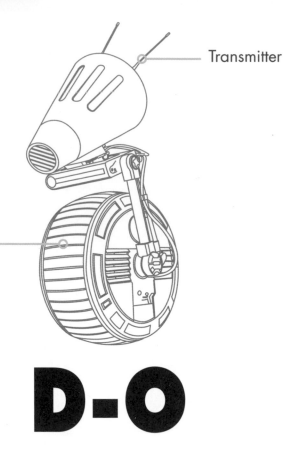

Transmitter

Uni-tread
wraps around
wheel

# D-O

**W**ho is this little, green-and-white droid? This is D-O. He is friendly and kind, but does sometimes get nervous. A mysterious and unknown droidsmith created D-O out of spare parts, so he is a completely unique droid. D-O adores the larger and braver BB-8, so rolls after him wherever he rolls, trying to copy the Resistance hero. He even talks to BB-8 using a simple form of droidspeak. This friendship inspires D-O to join the Resistance, too!

## D-O never falls over because a rebalancing device inside his single wheel keeps him upright!

Telescope eye

# BB-9E

**B**B-unit droids are usually quite friendly. Look at BB-8. He's a cheerful, helpful droid. But BB-9E is always unfriendly and suspicious. BB-9E works on a First Order command ship called the *Supremacy*. He patrols this starship making sure everything is in order. If his glowing red eye spots any trouble, then he alerts the authorities. He especially dislikes spies! Unfortunately, he isn't ever rewarded for his hard work. No wonder he's so bad-tempered!

**BB-9E once helped the First Order capture Resistance spies Finn and Rose. The droid wasted no time announcing their presence!**

Holoprojector

Useful tools
hidden inside

# CB-23

**D**on't mind CB-23 if she appears a little stern.
BB-8 thought this when he first met her.
But when BB-8 and CB-23 fought off some savage
monkey-lizards together, they became friends.
CB-23 is a BB-series droid, like BB-8. She can fire
cables and give enemy droids an electric shock.
Once, she had a fight with an enemy droid called
MB-13A. She tricked MB-13A into falling down
an elevator shaft. Well done, CB-23!

**If a BB-series droid has a dome-shaped
head with a flat top, like CB-23, then
they are called "bucket-heads."**

Powerful
antenna

Body
contains
tools

# BB-8

**S**ay hello to BB-8. He is a kind, playful droid
who always looks out for his friends. BB-8's
best friend is Poe Dameron, who is a talented pilot.
They fly in Poe's spaceship, an X-wing starfighter.
BB-8 sits in the copilot droid seat and helps Poe
navigate. On land, BB-8 can roll along very quickly.
His ball-shaped body turns while his head stays still.
He can roll at more than 13 mph (21 kph)—that's
faster than you would be on a bicycle. Go, BB-8!

**BB-8 uses a mini blowtorch tool for
repairs. When he's in a good mood,
it makes a perfect "thumbs up!"**

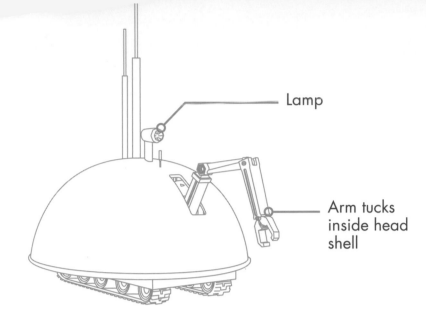

Lamp

Arm tucks inside head shell

# LIN-V8K MINING DROID

**T**ortoise-like mining droids like LIN-V8K have a thick, dome-shaped head for a reason. Mining is dangerous, and workers often need to blast holes in the mountains. They need mining droids to carry explosives for them! The droids' armored shells protect them from falling rocks. Mining droids roll along on caterpillar treads, which help them travel over bumpy ground. They can see through dust storms, fog, radiation, and even sand and earth.

**LIN-V8K once worked on a desert planet. Scavengers called Jawas found it and restored it and then tried to sell it.**

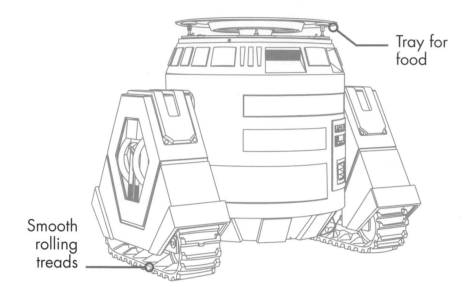

Tray for food

Smooth rolling treads

# PA-LT4

**S**ome droids fly starships and have epic space battles. Other droids serve food at parties. Can you guess which one PA-LT4 is? This polite, white-and-gold droid carries fresh fruit on a serving tray. PA-LT4 served food on board gangster Dryden Voss's luxurious space yacht. The droid moves silently around on rolling treads. But it is always careful not to get under anyone's feet. It knows there would be trouble if it tripped up a gangster.

**PA-LT4's serving tray is refrigerated, keeping anything it carries deliciously cool.**

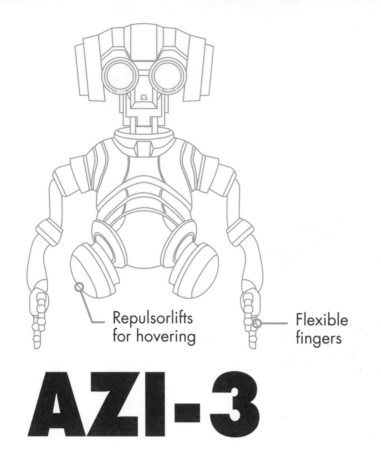

Repulsorlifts
for hovering

Flexible
fingers

# AZI-3

**A**ZI-3 is a flying medical droid. His full name is AZI-345211896246498721347. But a friendly soldier called Fives gave him the shorter name AZI-3. This droid works as a surgeon on a water world called Kamino, where an army of cloned soldiers is being created. AZI-3 and Fives uncover a secret about the clone army. Unknown to the clones, they have a computer chip put into their body. This means they can be controlled. AZI-3 believes that this is a bad thing, and he wants to let people know!

## AZI-3 can transform his body into an amazing speeder bike. Zoom!

Arms can give electric shocks!

Extra arm tucked away

# CHOPPER

**D**id you know that droids can be bad-tempered? They can! Take a look at C1-10P, known as Chopper. He is an old droid whose original parts have been replaced by second-hand ones. He doesn't like most other droids, and he isn't keen on humans or aliens either. But once he gets to know you, he can be a loyal team-member. He might still play mean tricks on you, though! Chopper prefers to play games rather than work, but he is also a rebel hero.

**Chopper flies a starship called the _Ghost_. He's made it so that he is the only one who can talk to the ship's computer!**

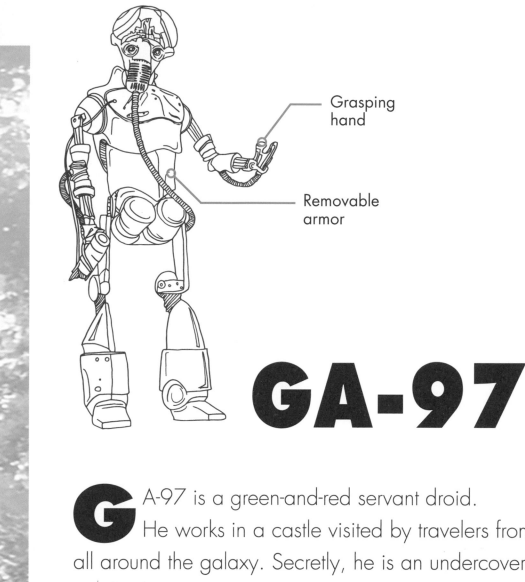

Grasping hand

Removable armor

# GA-97

**G**A-97 is a green-and-red servant droid. He works in a castle visited by travelers from all around the galaxy. Secretly, he is an undercover spy for the Resistance, the brave group that wants to stop the evil First Order. GA-97 is always listening. If he sees or hears anything interesting, he quickly sends a coded message into deep space. The signal is picked up by fellow droid friend C-3PO at the Resistance's secret base on another planet.

**GA-97's legs and arms can fold away inside his body. It's useful if he wants to hide in a big pile of scrap metal!**

Extra arms
and tools can
be added

# WED TREADWELL DROID

If you were lucky enough to own a starship, you might need some help to do repairs. Better get yourself a treadwell droid. They can have lots of arms, each with a different tool at the end. They trundle around on wheeled platforms and see using a sensor pole in the middle. These useful droids are found all over the galaxy repairing ships, droids, and other machines. But they can be fragile, so you need to look after them. If you do, they'll work for years.

**Treadwell droids sometimes chase insects, mistaking their whining noise for the sound of a faulty machine!**

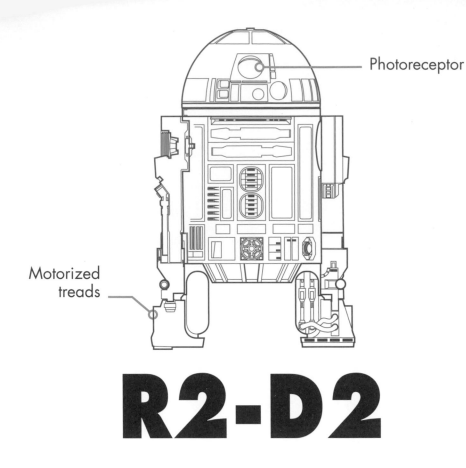

Photoreceptor

Motorized treads

# R2-D2

**T**his little droid is a true hero and helped save the galaxy! He is programmed to help pilots fly their spaceships, and he flew bravely on many missions with the Jedi Anakin Skywalker. Later, he flew in Luke Skywalker's X-wing starfighter, even going with Luke to the swamp planet Dagobah to meet Jedi Master Yoda. R2-D2 is quick-thinking in battle, and he never gives up! He talks in whistles and beeps, but he makes sure he is understood.

**R2-D2's body is small but full of surprises. All kinds of cool gadgets can pop out, including rocket boosters and a zapper!**

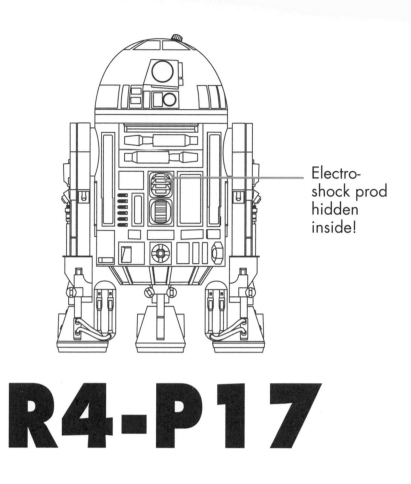

Electro-shock prod hidden inside!

# R4-P17

**R**4-P17, or "Arfour," is a red-and-white astromech droid. She works for a Jedi Knight called Obi-Wan Kenobi. They fly together in a red starfighter. Obi-Wan does not like flying, so he allows Arfour to take control of the ship. They go on many dangerous missions. Once, they had to fly through an area full of fast-moving space rocks. One wrong turn would have meant a crash that could have destroyed them and their ship. Luckily, brave Arfour got them out safely.

**If anyone tries to steal Obi-Wan's starfighter ship, Arfour gives them a little electric shock. Ouch!**

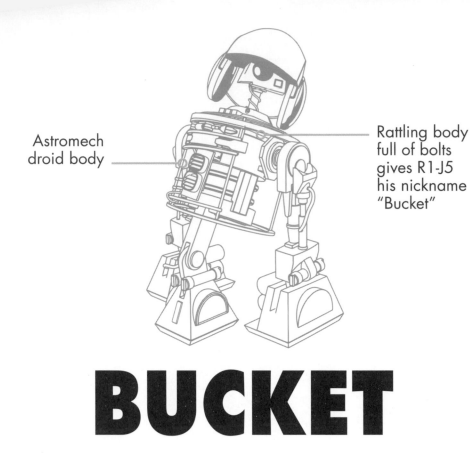

Astromech droid body

Rattling body full of bolts gives R1-J5 his nickname "Bucket"

# BUCKET

R1-J5 is known as Bucket. His prized possession is a pilot's helmet. He says he feels naked without it and isn't at all happy when BB-8 borrows it. Bucket often fights with BB-8, especially when BB-8 plays pranks on him. Bucket is a mechanic droid. He is also a copilot with a racer named Jarek Yeager. He respects great pilots, but he can be rude to rookie pilots. He often slams into them, or wakes them up with a loud alarm!

**Bucket is very good at playing darts. He usually hits the bullseye right on target. But one time he accidentally hit his copilot!**

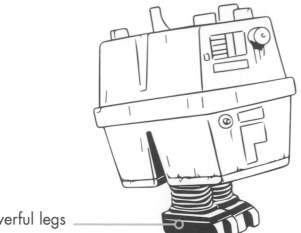

Powerful legs _____

# GONK DROID

**G**onk droids are a bit like walking batteries. They are found all over the galaxy, often in spaceports and garages, where they are used to recharge machines and vehicles. They have a variety of plug-in points around their bodies. Their true name is an EG-series power droid, but most people call them gonk droids because of the low honking sound they make as they walk: "gonk gonk!" Some are hundreds of years old, but they just keep on gonking!

**Gonk droids are cute but they aren't so smart. They can't really see where they are going and often get completely lost!**

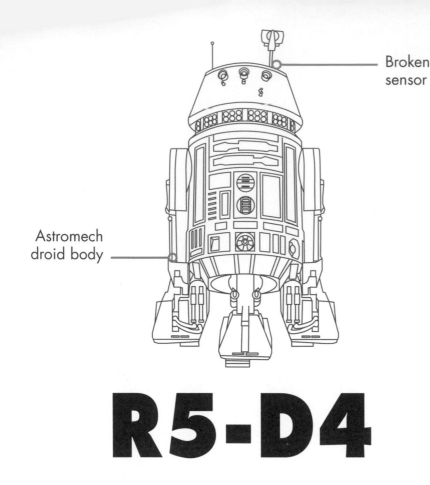

Broken sensor

Astromech droid body

# R5-D4

**R**5-D4 was owned by droid traders called Jawas on the desert planet Tatooine. Jawas travel around looking for people who want to buy their droids. One day, they met Luke Skywalker. Later, Luke Skywalker would become a famous Jedi and rebel pilot. But at that time he lived with his uncle and aunt on their farm. Luke and his uncle wanted to buy R5-D4. But unfortunately poor R5-D4's top blew up! So Luke bought another captured droid instead: R2-D2.

**Luke Skywalker called R5-D4 "Red" because of the red details on the droid's astromech body.**

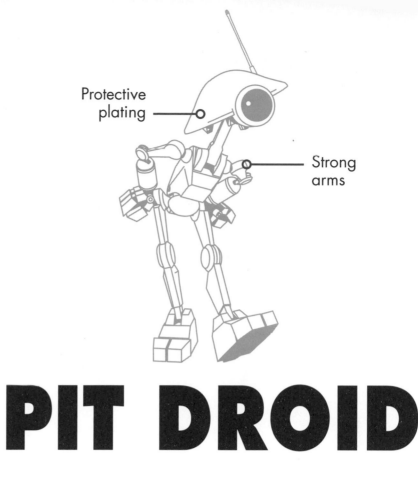

Protective plating

Strong arms

# PIT DROID

**O**n some planets, aliens race high-speed vehicles called podracers around a track with lots of twists and turns. This dangerous sport is called podracing. When a podracer breaks or needs more fuel, the pilot pulls their vehicle over to an area at the side of the track called a pit. There, little pit droids are ready and waiting to help look after the podracers. These droids are very useful, but are easily excited and often get into trouble.

**There's a clever solution if a pit droid is causing mischief. If you tap one on its head, it will fold itself away!**

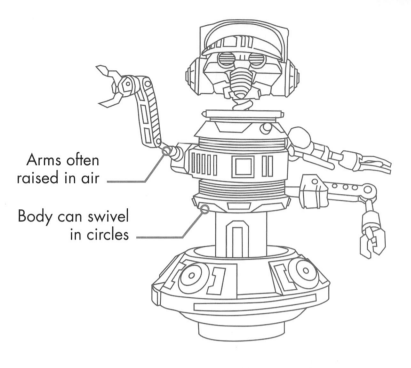

Arms often raised in air

Body can swivel in circles

# DJ R3X

In some parts of the galaxy, droids are not allowed inside cantinas. But on the planet Batuu, a droid is the in-house DJ in Oga's Cantina! The droid is called R3X, but you can call him Rex. He used to be a pilot droid, but he crash landed on Batuu and was reprogrammed as a DJ. He even wears headphones! He's quite a sight in his brightly lit DJ booth. His head can pop up and down on a telescopic neck. He is a party machine!

**R3X used to pilot a shuttle, taking passengers on short trips to nearby planets.**

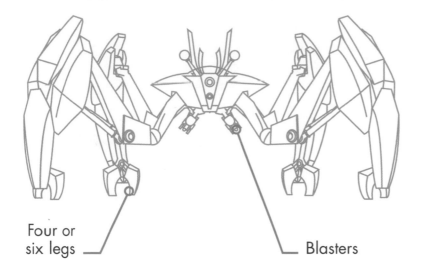

Four or six legs — Blasters

# CRAB DROID

These droids look like living creatures, and are the biggest crabs you'll ever see. They scuttle along on either four or six legs and they have heads with glowing red eyes. But don't be fooled—crab droids are machines and they are dangerous! Their legs aren't just used for walking. They can also raise them in the air and—whomp!—crush anything in their way. Their limbs have sharp pincers at the end. Worst of all, they have blasters attached under their heads.

**Crab droids' two front legs can suck up swamp mud and then spray it out. That's why they are also called muckrakers!**

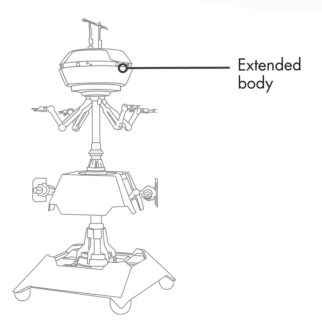

Extended body

# FIRST ORDER SENTRY DROID

**D**on't be fooled by this droid. It looks like a harmless pile of boxes, rolling slowly around. But if you're an intruder, it springs into action. Its head and body lift apart and arms with blasters pop out. Sentry droids work for the First Order, a group trying to take over the galaxy. Their job is to guard bases, space stations, and ships. Many patroled the First Order's secret planet, Starkiller Base, and the *Finalizer*, Kylo Ren and General Hux's ship.

**A sentry droid once surprised BB-8 and his friends at a deserted base when it burst up out of its box with weapons buzzing!**

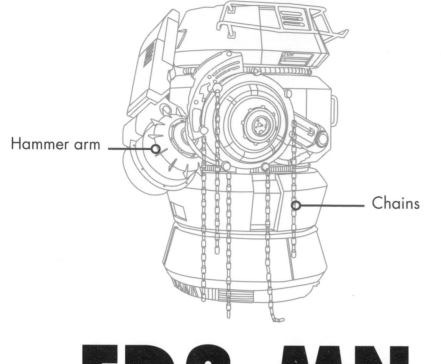

Hammer arm

Chains

# FD3-MN

On some planets, venues open their doors to smugglers and pirates who want to relax and play games. On the planet Vandor, one particular cantina owner even allows droid fighting. In this rough sport, droids are made to attack each other for entertainment. FD3-MN is one of these fighting droids. Her powerful arms can be fitted with saws and a range of other weapons. FD3-MN likes fighting and is popular with the gathered crowds. If she wins, then the watchers might also win a prize!

**FD3-MN fighting droids are also known as gladiator droids.**

Arms take samples of land on other planets

# IMPERIAL PROBE DROID

**T**his small but skillful droid never gives up! Its job is to seek and find people. Darth Vader sends thousands of probe droids all over the galaxy to work for him. They travel inside tiny spaceships called hyperdrive pods. After reaching a planet, probe droids fly around looking for signs of their target. They move almost silently, with big eyes and cameras to scan and record what they see. When they find the target, they send word back to Vader at once.

**If a probe droid thinks it is in danger, it has a blaster for defense. But if the threat is too great, then it self-destructs!**

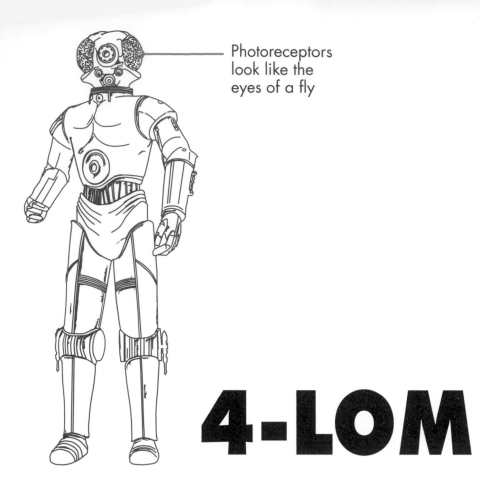

Photoreceptors look like the eyes of a fly

# 4-LOM

**T**his battered, rusty droid was once a clean, shiny droid. He worked on a luxury passenger spaceship. His masters were insectlike aliens with large eyes. That's why 4-LOM also has an insectlike face— it helped him fit in. Something went wrong with his programming, though, and 4-LOM became a criminal bounty hunter. He is hired to hunt for people. If he finds them, he gets paid—that's called a bounty. 4-LOM is one of the most successful bounty hunters in the galaxy.

**4-LOM will work for anyone, even evil Darth Vader, as long as they pay him at the end of the mission!**

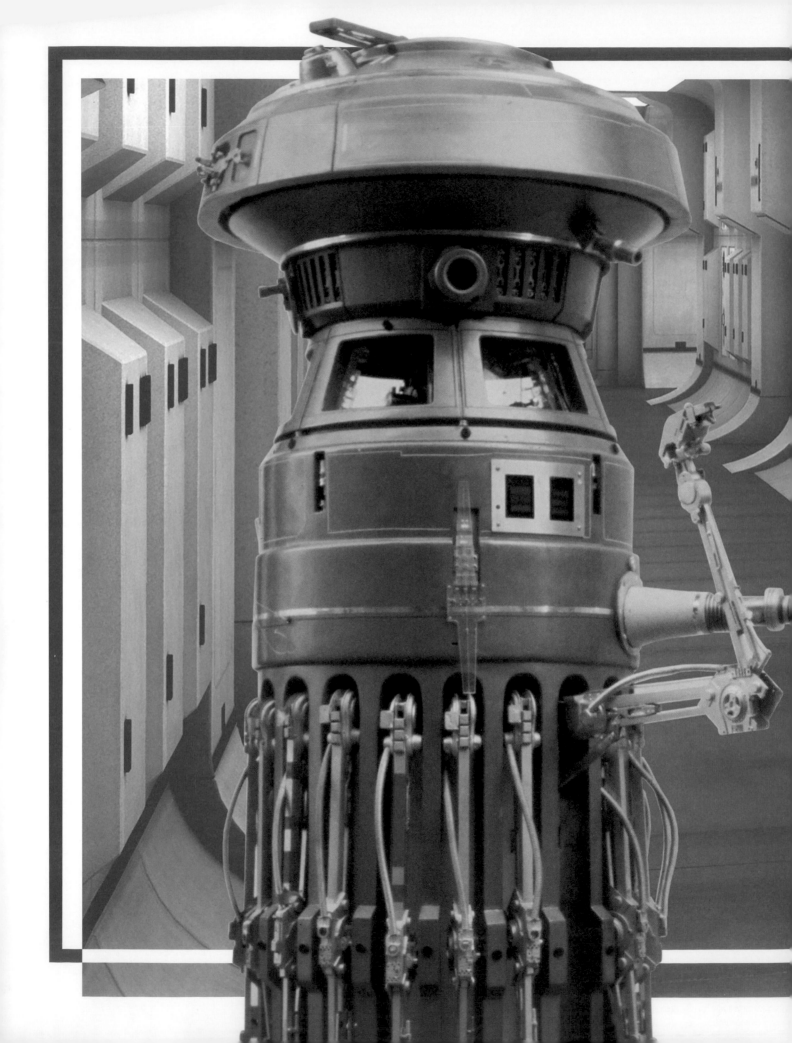

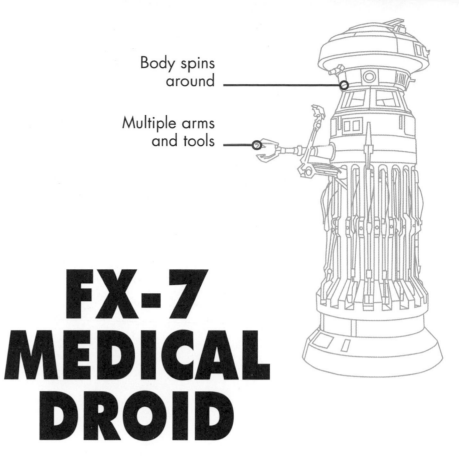

Body spins around

Multiple arms and tools

# FX-7 MEDICAL DROID

If you were injured, you would be glad to see an FX-series medical assistant droid. These droids use their many arms to check your condition. They are programmed to treat all kinds of alien species. They use their superior droid brains to choose the best treatment. If they decide you need surgery, they will work fast with a surgeon droid. If your wounds just need healing, they might put you in a bacta tank—a large basin of special fluid that repairs damaged skin.

**An FX-series medical droid helped mend Darth Vader when he was transforming into a cyborg (a mix of man and machine)!**

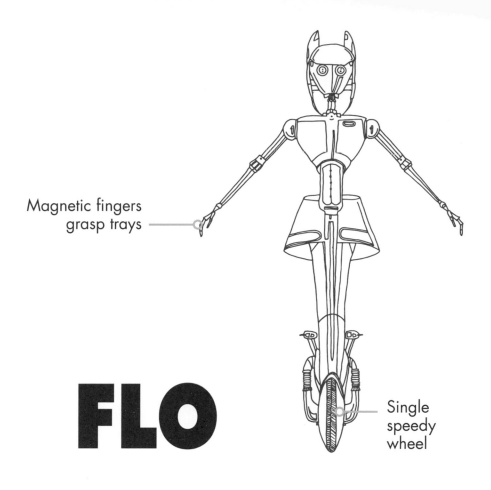

Magnetic fingers
grasp trays

Single
speedy
wheel

# FLO

**A** WA-7 droid is a type of waiter droid found in restaurants and cafés across the galaxy. FLO is the nickname of an antique WA-7 droid that works in Dexter's Diner on the city planet Coruscant. Dexter is the four-armed alien who runs the place. FLO is great at her job. She whizzes between the tables carrying drinks and plates of greasy food. Well-behaved regulars at the diner receive a cheerful greeting from FLO. Sometimes her customers include Jedi and other important, hungry passers-by.

**FLO knows what her customers'
favorite drink is—Jawa Juice!**

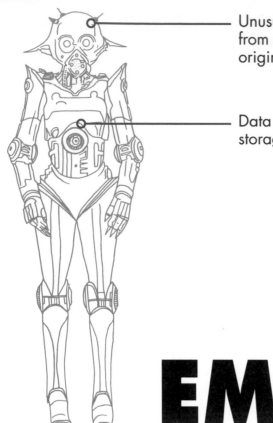

Unusual parts from mysterious origins

Data storage

# EMMIE

**M**E-8D9 is known as Emmie. She is a very old droid, and nobody is quite sure who originally built her. Now she lives with an alien called Maz in a castle on far-away planet, Takodana. Emmie helps Maz run her castle, which can get very busy. Many alien and droid travelers stay at the castle on their way across the galaxy. Emmie speaks many different languages, so she often translates for aliens who don't understand each other.

**Emmie has a special way to break up fights. She can fire electric darts from her pointy finger tips. Watch out!**

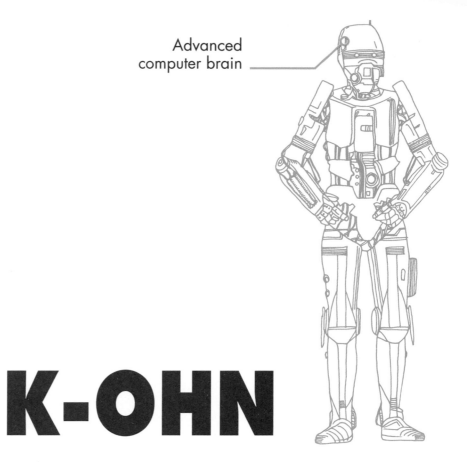

Advanced
computer brain

# K-OHN

**M**ost droids are owned by somebody.
But a few lucky ones are free to do as they
please. K-OHN is a free droid. He is a L-1 tactical
droid. These droids have powerful processors to help
with difficult tasks, such as planning a battle. But now
K-OHN sells his skills to whoever will pay him.
He plans to use the money to improve his brain even
further. But he will have to wait, because upgrades
are not cheap and he likes to share his earnings
with a band of street urchins. Kind K-OHN!

**K-OHN wants to upgrade his brain
so that he can understand religious beliefs.**

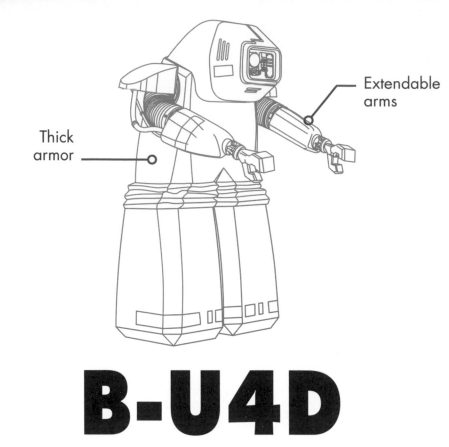

Thick armor

Extendable arms

# B-U4D

**W**hen you need to lift something heavy, call on B-U4D, or Buford as he is often known. B-U4D is a loading droid and can be found working on ships in starship hangars. He helps the Resistance, which is fighting the evil First Order. The Resistance treats its droids well. Buford's heavy-duty claws can grab hold of spaceship parts and fuel tanks that are much heavier than he is. Busy Buford doesn't have time for chatting. He likes to get on with the job.

**Unfortunately, Buford's vision is poor. That's why he's painted bright yellow—so you can see him and get out of his way!**

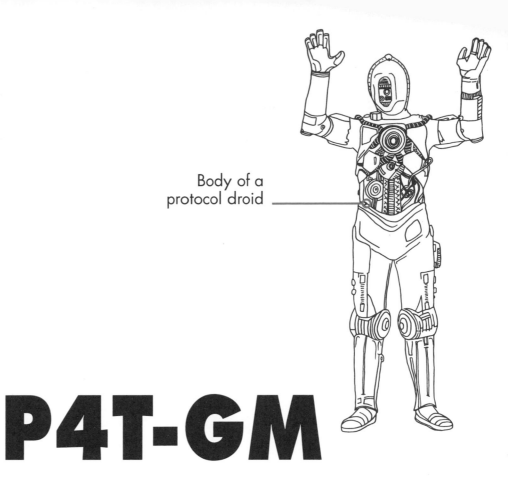

Body of a protocol droid

# P4T-GM

**W**orking in a dangerous mine such as the one on planet Kessel is an unpleasant job. Many droids are forced to work there. They work long hours, handling harsh materials, and never receive a relaxing oil bath to clean their joints. So it's not surprising that arguments and even fights break out. That's when P4T-GM must step in. P4T-GM is programmed to resolve conflicts. Its usual advice is to "sort it out later, on your own time!"

**P4T-GM has so much work to do that sometimes it throws its hands in the air and gives up! It's a hard life being a droid.**

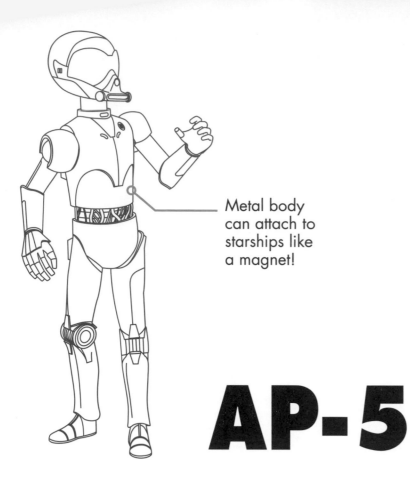

Metal body can attach to starships like a magnet!

# AP-5

AP-5 has a blue metallic body and a head shaped like an insect. He used to work for the Empire and the evil rulers led by Darth Vader. AP-5's masters did not treat him kindly, and it made him very grumpy. But everything changed for AP-5 when he managed to escape! He joined the rebels, a group that was fighting against Darth Vader. AP-5 is now friends with a rebel droid named Chopper. They are both grumpy so they get along.

**The rebels were happy when AP-5 joined them. He could share lots of the Empire's secrets with his new rebel friends.**

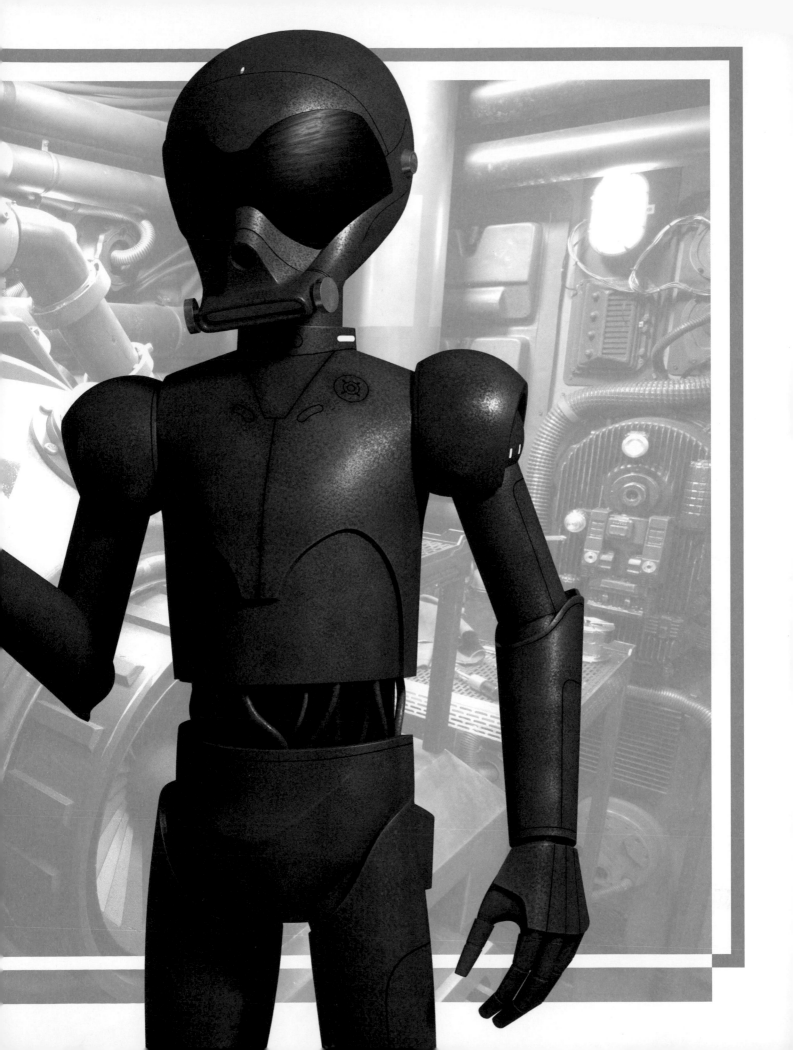

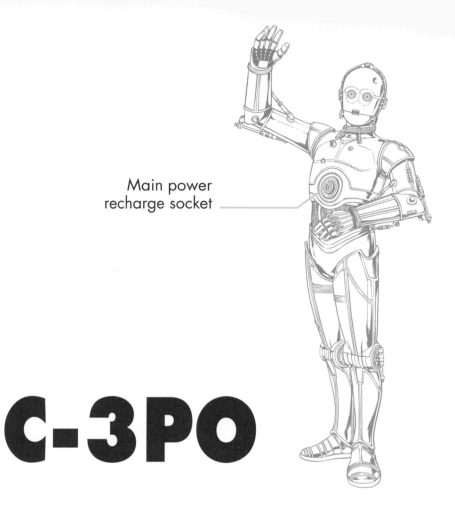

Main power
recharge socket

# C-3PO

**T**his golden droid is named C-3PO. He is a good friend to have by your side when you travel the galaxy. He speaks more than seven million languages, so he can help you talk to aliens and creatures from many planets. Although he is a good communicator, C-3PO often panics! It's lucky that his best friend is another droid called R2-D2, who is fearless and resourceful. They make a good team and often end up going on missions together.

**C-3PO keeps himself shiny and clean. It's hard to believe that he was built using scraps from other droids!**

Shiny finish
matches shiny
Canto Bight

# SE8 WAITER DROID

In the galaxy's top restaurants and nightspots, SE8 waiter droids zigzag through the crowds. These useful droids are designed to work with people. The SE8 is a professional model, trusted to work at even the most lavish parties in the glamorous city Canto Bight. While carefully balancing trays of drinks, motors in their bodies help them avoid knocking into anyone. A light at the center on their chests changes color to show which delicious drinks they are serving.

**Humanlike service droids are common across the galaxy with many different jobs, including cook and baker droids!**

Astromech
droid head

Power cell

# L3-37

L3-37 is a very smart pilot droid. She works alongside a human pilot, a smuggler named Lando. Together they fly a famous starship called the *Millennium Falcon*. L3 cares a lot about other droids. She thinks they should never work as slaves. On one mission with Lando, she helps free many droids from working in a dangerous mine. Sadly, L3 is badly damaged, so Lando puts her brain into the *Millennium Falcon*. L3 now lives on as part of the ship!

**Some droids are one of a kind.
L3-37 built herself from scraps
of old and broken droids!**

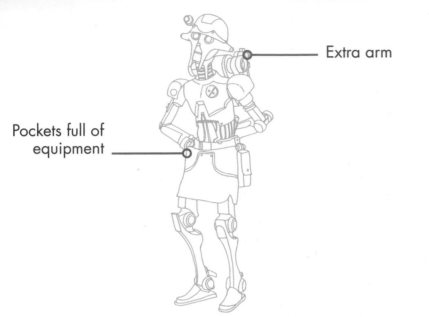

Extra arm

Pockets full of equipment

# PROFESSOR HUYANG

Huyang is an old droid professor. He is an architect droid, desgined to help build things. For over a thousand years, as far as Huyang can count, he has helped teach children to become Jedi. He even taught wise Master Yoda! One of his most important lessons is how to build a lightsaber. Each Jedi must find their own unique style. Huyang takes his students to a planet to find special kyber crystals, which will power their lightsabers.

**Once, some pirates knocked off Huyang's head and his arms. Luckily, his Jedi students were able to rebuild him.**

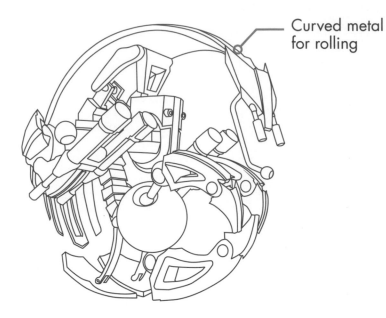

Curved metal for rolling

# DROIDEKA

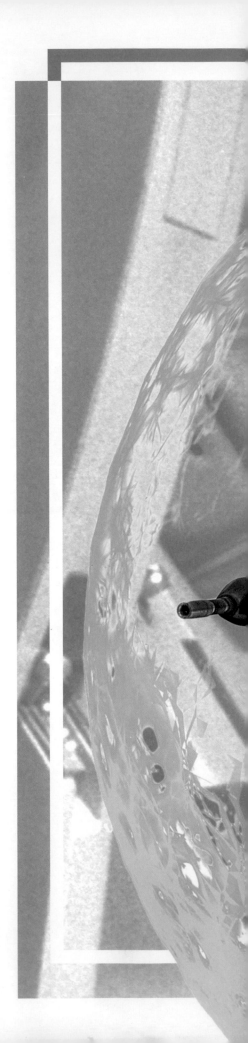

**T**he first time you see a droideka, you might not realize it's a droid at all! You will see a metal ball zooming toward you at top speed. When it stops, it will unroll into standing position, revealing three legs and two arms. Each arm has a blaster on the end. The droid is protected inside a glowing blue bubble, called an energy shield. Anything fired at it will bounce right off. However, slow-moving objects, such as a lightsaber, can pierce the shield.

**Droidekas roll very fast. Much faster than a person can run and, sometimes, faster than a car on a freeway!**

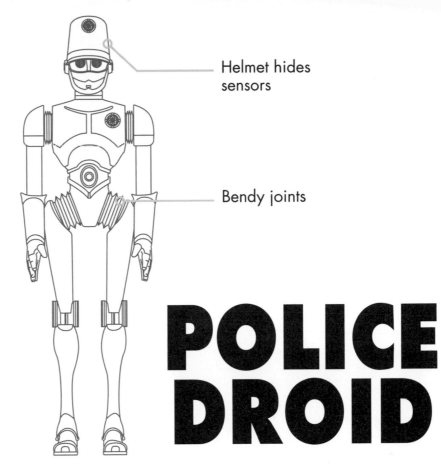

Helmet hides sensors

Bendy joints

# POLICE DROID

**H**ere come the droid police! These guardian droids wear tall hats with a police symbol on the front. This symbol is also on their blue-gray armor. Police droids help keep the peace on the galaxy's capital planet, Coruscant. They patrol the streets on foot or on speeder bikes. Some pilot airspeeders, which can carry prisoners in a secure section at the back. Police droids must be ready at all times, so they carry blasters and batons for defense.

**Police droids like to drink a cup of hot oil through their small mouths. It helps keep them awake!**

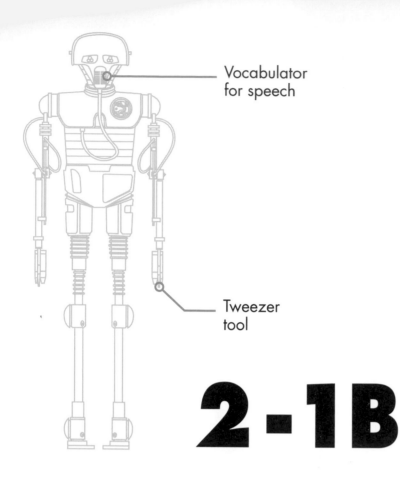

Vocabulator
for speech

Tweezer
tool

# 2·1B

**T**his 2-1B medical droid is an excellent doctor. If you need surgery, a 2-1B will perform it. Their arms can be fitted with mechanical hands or other medical equipment. They can even have a needle arm fitted if you need an injection. 2-1Bs have worked with humans for a long time. They are programmed with lots of medical knowledge. Twice when Jedi Luke Skywalker was injured, one particular 2-1B treated him—and saved his life both times!

**When Luke Skywalker was injured the second time, he asked for 2-1B to be his doctor because he's such a caring droid!**

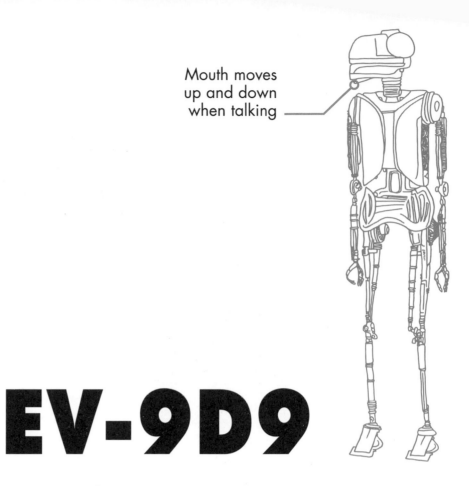

Mouth moves
up and down
when talking

# EV-9D9

In a palace on the desert planet Tatooine lives a powerful gang boss called Jabba the Hutt. Droids and other servants wait on Jabba, doing whatever he asks. In the cellars of the palace works EV-9D9, a droid that used to be good but has gone bad. EV-9D9 frightens all the servant droids into doing their jobs. She hangs droids upside down to punish them. She even pulls them apart. Whatever you do, stay away from EV-9D9!

**EV-9D9 forced C-3PO to be Jabba's translator. She also made R2-D2 serve drinks to his guests. How humiliating!**

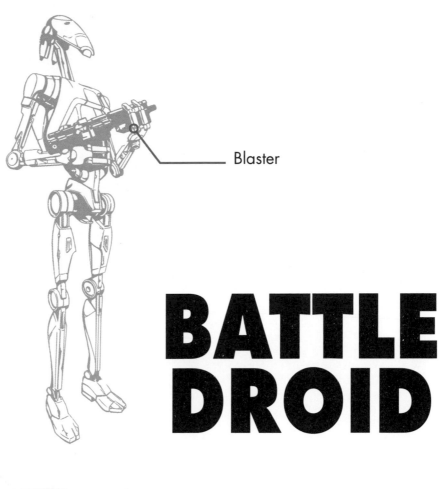

Blaster

# BATTLE DROID

**T**hese clanking mechanical soldiers are battle droids. They are simple machines and are easily confused. They cannot think for themselves—a big computer on a starship tells them what to do. If the computer shuts down, all the battle droids shut down, too. Battle droids say "roger, roger" to show that they understand a command. If things are going wrong, they say "uh-oh." One battle droid on its own is not that powerful. But many together make a strong army.

**Some battle droids pilot flying vehicles called Single Trooper Aerial Platforms. These are big enough for just one droid.**

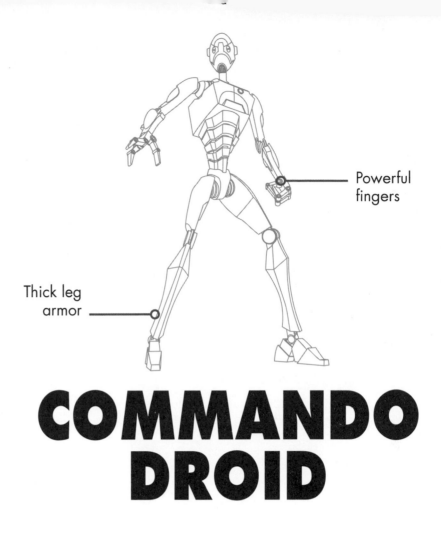

Powerful fingers

Thick leg armor

# COMMANDO DROID

**B**X-series commando droids are battle droids with brain modules! They are tougher and better at fighting than ordinary battle droids. They are also much more athletic, with faster reflexes. Commando droids go on dangerous, undercover missions. They sometimes disguise themselves as the enemy and can even mimic their voices. But they can't completely hide their robotic movements, which usually give them away!

**Commando droids have enough strength to lift a human soldier off the ground.**

Sensor

# SUPER BATTLE DROID

**S**uper battle droids are taller than a fully grown human. They are covered in thick armor, which makes them fearless in battle. They have powerful blasters on their wrists, and their arms are strong enough to lift another soldier right off the ground. Yet their brain processors are quite basic. They don't always know what to do in battle. Even a small droid like R2-D2 can defeat a super battle droid. Just because you're big, doesn't mean you're the best!

**Despite their height and weight, some super battle droids can fly using jetpacks!**

97

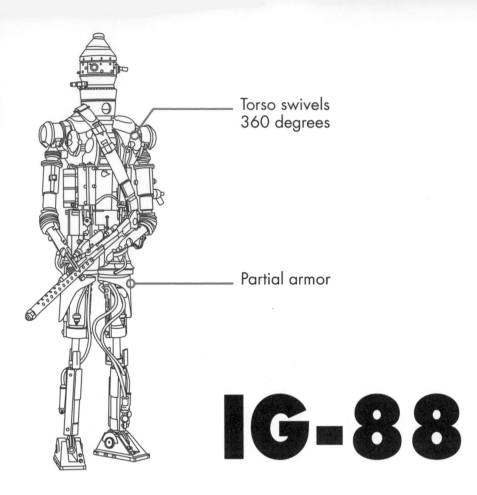

Torso swivels
360 degrees

Partial armor

# IG-88

This walking heap of scrap metal gives droids a bad name. IG-88 was designed to be a soldier droid. But from the moment he was activated, he chose a life of crime. IG-88 is armed and very dangerous. All he wants to do is to hunt and destroy. He doesn't mind who hires him—it could be a crime lord or Darth Vader himself—as long as he gets paid. He prefers to work alone, and can't be trusted in a team. He'll betray his partner if offered the right price.

**The lights on IG-88's head allow him to see in all directions at once. There's no hiding from this droid.**

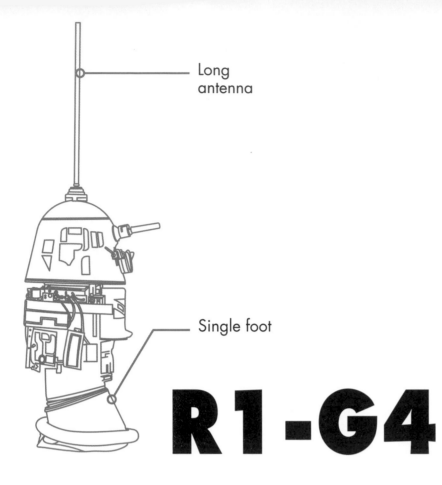

Long antenna

Single foot

# R1-G4

**T**his is one of the oldest models of droid in the galaxy. Like R2-D2, R1-G4 is an astromech droid, designed to help pilots in space. But it is so large, it can only be used on the biggest starships. Somehow, R1-G4 ended up far away, abandoned on a desert planet after the owner of its ship was captured. Some creatures called Jawas found R1-G4 and tried to sell it to some farmers—even though they knew that it was not designed to help on a farm!

**R1 droids were the first droids to be able to talk in droidspeak. Beep boop!**

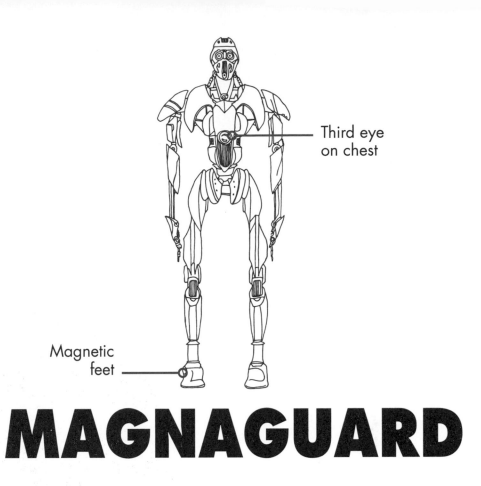

Third eye on chest

Magnetic feet

# MAGNAGUARD

Emperors and generals often have bodyguards. They may not always need them, but it helps them look important! Some guards are droids, like these steely MagnaGuards. Evil leader General Grievous keeps MagnaGuards and uses them to fight for him. Grievous wears a cloak and so do his bodyguards. Their droid bodies are battered and their cloaks are torn from battles. Grievous thinks this makes them look mean and tough!

**MagnaGuards fight with long electric poles called electrostaffs. These weapons can block any attack—including lightsabers!**

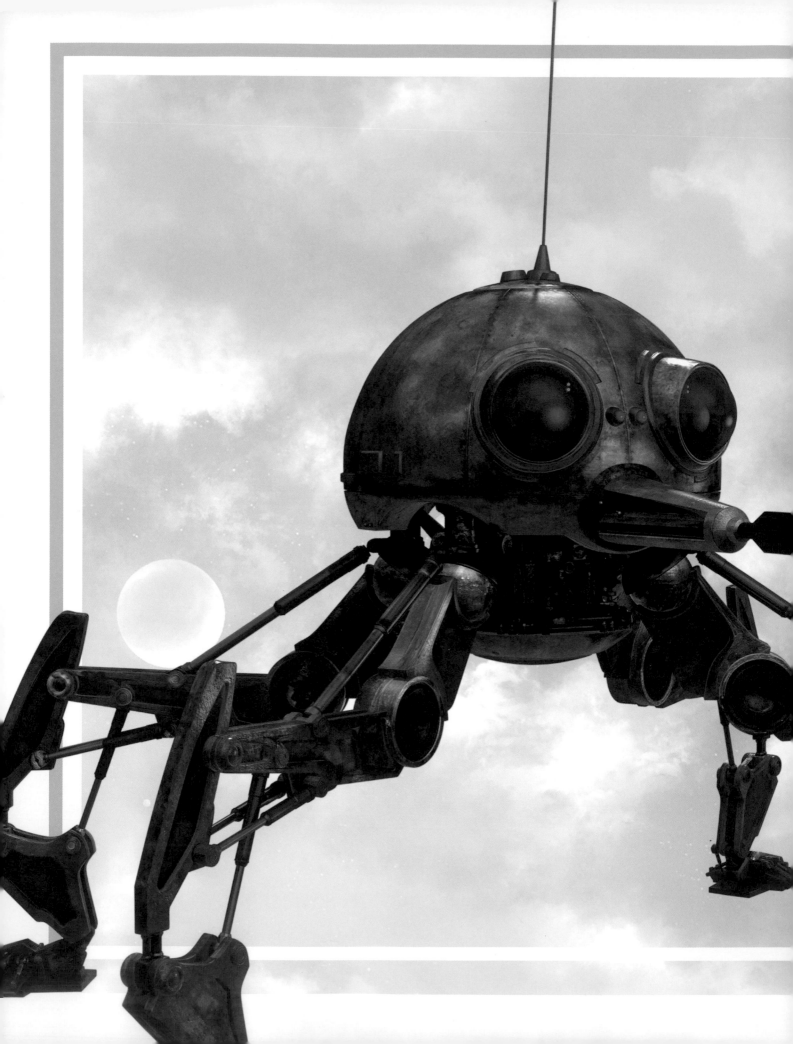

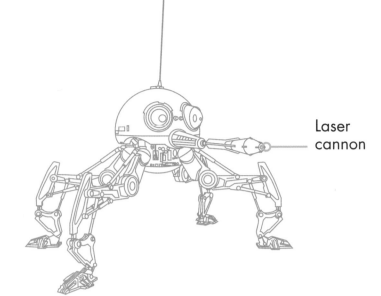

Laser cannon

# DWARF SPIDER DROID

These droids scuttle around on four legs, looking for something to blow up. They can run fast and climb up and down walls and cliffs. When they are not fighting on a battlefield, they work underground as guards in mines. Their red headlamp eyes light up the dark. Facing a dwarf spider droid in battle is dangerous, as it has a laser cannon attached to the front of its head. But it can only fire forward. So if you're quick, you can run around behind it and defeat it!

**When threatened, dwarf spider droids self-destruct!**

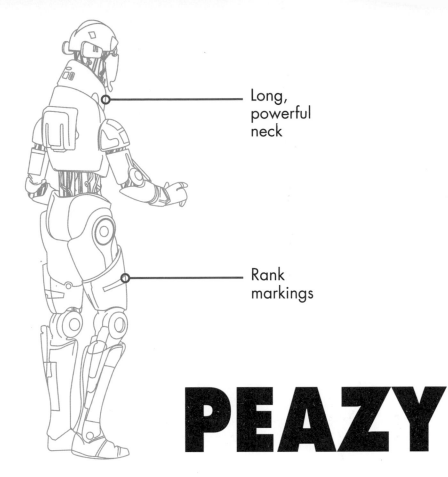

Long, powerful neck

Rank markings

# PEAZY

**T**his blue droid is called PZ-4CO, or Peazy for short. She is a member of the Resistance and works on a secret base. The Resistance is trying to save the galaxy from the evil First Order. She talks to other droids scattered across the galaxy. These droids look for signs of the First Order and send reports to Peazy. She then builds up a map of the First Order's movements. When the First Order discovers the secret base, Peazy helps everyone escape.

**Peazy also offers first aid to anyone who is hurt. Her friendly voice helps people feel calmer right away!**

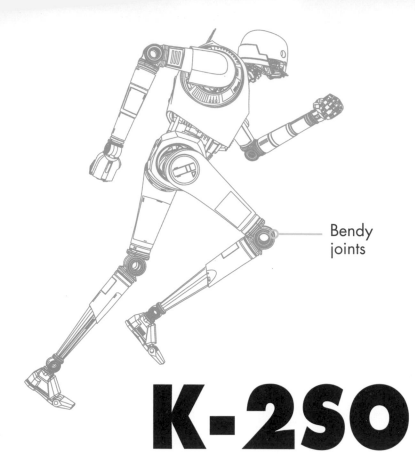

Bendy joints

# K-2SO

**A** droid can switch sides. K-2SO was created as a fierce droid for the Empire, the evil rulers of the galaxy. But he was found by some rebels, who were trying to stop the Empire. The rebels reprogrammed him, so now he works with them. Other rebels get a shock when they first meet him, as he still looks like a mean droid working for the other side. But he is a loyal soldier for the rebels. He is also a great spy because he blends in with the Empire's forces.

**K-2SO has a habit of always speaking his mind, even if it's not a kind comment. Nothing will stop him from being honest.**

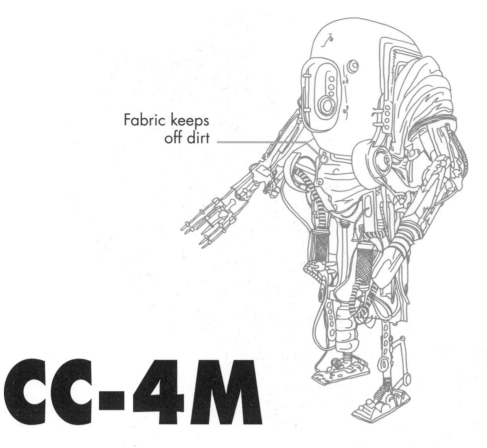

Fabric keeps off dirt

# CC-4M

CC-4M is a heavy-duty loadlifter droid who works in a mine on the planet Kessel. The mine is run by a criminal gang that forces workers to dig a valuable rock from the mines. Loadlifter droids like CC-4M carry huge crates of rock up from the mine. The dust and dirt clogs up their parts, so they often malfunction. CC-4M used to be the leader of a team of construction droids on an ice moon. He misses his friends in his old team.

**CC-4M joined some other droids when a rebellion started in the Kessel mines. Now he is a free droid!**

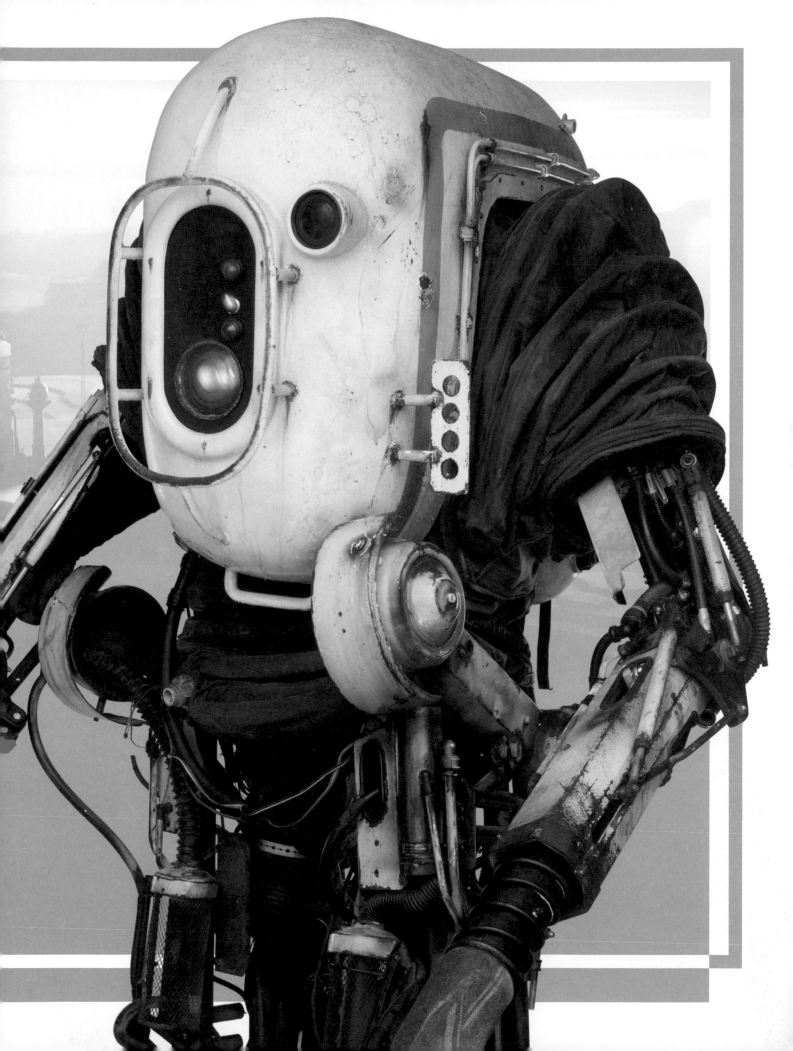

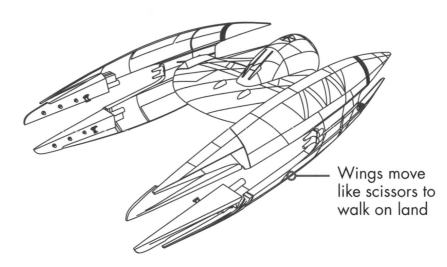

Wings move like scissors to walk on land

# VULTURE DROID

Is it a droid? Is it a starship? Vulture droids are both! They can fly through space without a pilot because they are controlled by a computer. They can also make faster turns than a pilot ever could. They fire from blasters on each wing. When a vulture droid lands on a planet, its wings transfom into legs so it can walk. Its head lifts up on a necklike stalk so its red eyes start seeking out its prey. On land or in space, the vulture rules!

**Vulture droids can talk to each other in a special droid language.**

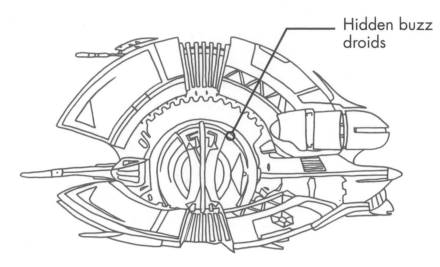

Hidden buzz droids

# DROID TRI-FIGHTER

**T**ri-fighters are droid starships—no pilot needed. Instead, they have an onboard brain module that helps them fly and attack. These ships are a menace to Jedi everywhere. They have a cannon weapon on each of their three curved wings and one larger cannon in the middle. In space, tri-fighters twist and turn at breathtaking speeds. They are entirely fearless and fly right into dangers that no living pilot would dare face.

**The tri-fighter is designed to look like the skull of a fierce prehistoric creature called a maygorr, from the planet Colla IV.**

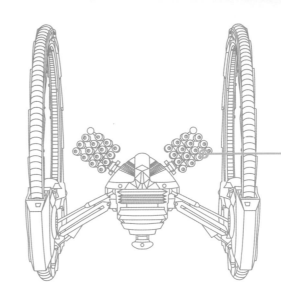

30 weapons attached on top

# HAILFIRE DROID

**Y**ou can't miss one of these tanks rolling into action on the battlefield. Their enormous hoop wheels are 6.8 meters (22 feet) tall—that's the height of a three-story building. They can roll at high speeds while firing missiles up into the air. A dirty cloud of black smoke trails behind each missile. The droid's brain is protected inside the pod in the center. A single red eye stares out at the front. You'd better get out of range before it spots you!

**A hailfire droid's pair of large wheels give it its nickname "wheel droid."**

# GLOSSARY

**Alien**
Someone who is not a human.

**Anakin Skywalker**
A powerful Jedi who turned evil and became Darth Vader.

**Antenna**
A rod or pole that sends and receives video and sound messages.

**Astromech droid**
A type of robot that repairs and helps fly a spaceship.

**Base**
The center of operations for an army or military group.

**Blaster**
A weapon that fires a blast of energy.

**Bounty hunter**
A person or droid who is paid to capture or kill someone else.

**Clone**
An exact copy of another person or thing.

**Command ship**
The largest ship in a group of starships. The leader of an army usually travels on the command ship.

**Copilot**
The second pilot in a starship or other vehicle.

**Darth Vader**
An evil man who wore a black helmet and face mask. He ruled the galaxy and fought with a lightsaber with a red blade.

**Death Star**
A deadly weapon in space. It looks like a planet with a huge firing weapon on one side.

**Droid**
A robot or mechanical being with a computer brain.

**Droidspeak**
The language spoken by some droids. It often sounds like beeps and whistles.

**The Empire**
Powerful, evil rulers of the galaxy. They took over from the peaceful rulers of the galaxy.

**First Order**
An evil group that wants to rule the galaxy after the Empire.

**Galaxy**
A massive collection of stars, planets, moons, and other objects in space.

**Gangster**
A member of a gang of violent criminals.

**Holoprojector**
A special device for showing three-dimensional images of people or things.

**Jawa**
Short creatures with glowing eyes. They travel around in groups and collect and sell droids and other machines.

## Jedi
Someone who learns to use a powerful invisible energy called the Force. Jedi are also trained to use a lightsaber.

## Jedi Knight
A Jedi who has completed their training and passed some special tests.

## Jetpack
A small, rocket-powered machine that allows a person (or a droid) to fly.

## Lightsaber
A sword that the Jedi use. The blade is made of a colorful glowing energy.

## Luke Skywalker
One of the greatest Jedi ever. He helped defeat the evil Empire, even though his own father was Darth Vader.

## Photoreceptor
A droid's eye. Droids may have one, two, three, or more photoreceptors. Some have them on their bodies instead of their heads!

## Radiation
Light and heat energy produced by living beings, machines, and stars. Some forms of radiation can be harmful.

## Rebels
Also known as the Rebel Alliance. This group worked hard to free the galaxy from the evil rulers called the Empire.

## Resistance
A team of people who are trying to save the galaxy from an evil group called the First Order.

## Scavenger
Someone who looks for things that someone else has thrown away, which they can use or sell.

## Shuttle
A transport vehicle that travels regularly between two places.

## Starfighter
A small, fast starship. They are usually flown by one pilot and a droid copilot.

## Starkiller Base
An ice planet that the First Order turned into a powerful weapon.

## Treads
Some droid's feet. They are often made of wheels. Some may be caterpillar or tank tracks (wheels that turn a looped belt of tracks).

## X-wing
A speedy starfighter with x-shaped wings, often flown by the Rebels and the Resistance.

# HEIGHT INDEX

From smallest to biggest, read about how the droids of the galaxy measure up against each other with this handy visual guide. Which one is your favorite?

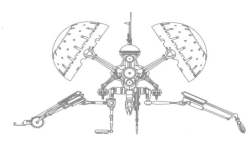

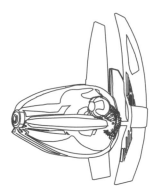

**Buzz Droid, page 10**

**Height:** 0.25m (10in) diameter
**Function:** Attacking ships in space

**DRK-1 Probe Droid, page 12**

**Height:** 0.3m (1ft)
**Function:** Sith missions

**ASN Courier Droid, page 14**

**Height:** 0.38m (1ft 3in)
**Function:** Carrying information or weapons

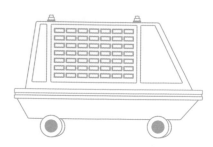

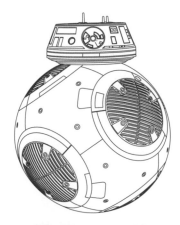

**Mouse Droid, page 16**

**Height:** 0.4m (1ft 4in)
**Function:** Repairing and cleaning starships

**D-O, page 18**

**Height:** 0.46m (1ft 6in) including antenna
**Function:** Unknown

**BB-9E, page 20**

**Height:** 0.6m (1ft 11in)
**Function:** Protecting First Order bases and starships

**CB-23, page 22**
Height: 0.67m (2ft 2in)
Function: Copiloting
Resistance ships

**BB-8, page 24**
Height: 0.67m (2ft 2in)
Function: Resistance missions

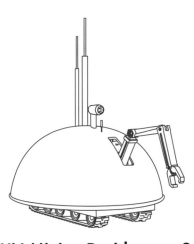

**LIN Mining Droid, page 26**
Height: 0.7m (2ft 4in) including antenna
Function: Planting explosions and
clearing debris from mines

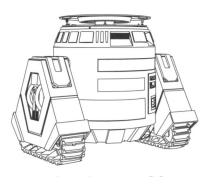

**PA-LT4, page 28**
Height: 0.84m (2ft 9in)
Function: Serving food and drinks

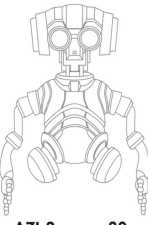

**AZI-3, page 30**
Height: 0.9m (2ft 11in)
Function: Medical assistance

**Chopper, page 32**
Height: 0.99m (3ft 2in)
Function: Maintaining the *Ghost*

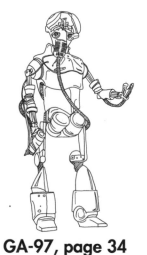

**GA-97, page 34**
Height: 1m (3ft 3in)
Function: Spy for the Resistance

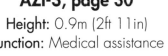

**WED Treadwell, page 36**
Height: 1m (3ft 3in)
Function: Repairing machinery

**R2-D2, page 38**
Height: 1.09m (3ft 6in)
Function: Rebel missions

**R4-P17, page 40**
Height: 1.09m (3ft 6in)
Function: Flying with Obi-Wan

**Bucket, page 42**
Height: 1.1m (3ft 7in)
Function: Copiloting races

**Gonk Droid, page 44**
Height: 1.1m (3ft 7in)
Function: Powering up vehicles

**R5-D4, page 46**
Height: 1.17m (3ft 10in)
Function: Astromech droid

**Pit Droid, page 48**
Height: 1.19m (3ft 11in)
Function: Fixing podracers

**DJ R3X, page 50**
Height: 1.26m (4ft 1in)
Function: Musical entertainment

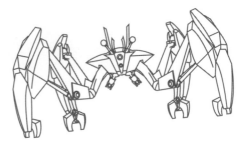

**Crab Droid, page 52**
Height: 1.49m (4ft 10in)
Function: Battle tank for navigating swampy ground

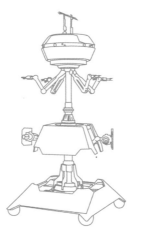

**First Order Sentry Droid, page 54**
Height: 1.5m (4ft 11in)
fully extended
Function: Defending First Order bases

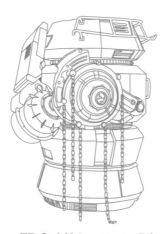

**FD3-MN, page 56**
Height: 1.52m (5ft)
Function: Fighting other droids in gladiator fights

### Imperial Probe Droid, page 58

**Height:** 1.6m (5ft 3in)

**Function:** Exploring planets

### 4-LOM, page 60

**Height:** 1.67m (5ft 5in)

**Function:** Bounty hunter

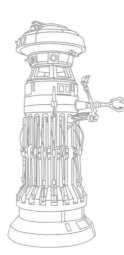

### FX-7, page 62

**Height:** 1.7m (5ft 6in)

**Function:** Medical aid

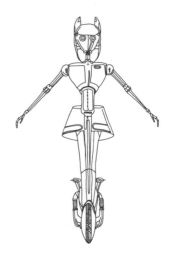

### FLO, page 64

**Height:** 1.7m (5ft 6in)

**Function:** Serving diner food

### Emmie, page 66

**Height:** 1.72m (5ft 7in)

**Function:** Translator

### K-0HN, page 68

**Height:** 1.75m (5ft 8in)

**Function:** Technical assistance

### B-U4D, page 70

**Height:** 1.75m (5ft 8in)

**Function:** Loading ships

### P4T-GM, page 72

**Height:** 1.75m (5ft 9in)

**Function:** Peacekeeper

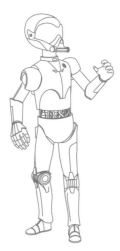

### AP-5, page 74

**Height:** 1.77m (5ft 10in)

**Function:** Gathering information

### C-3PO, page 76

**Height:** 1.77m (5ft 10in)

**Function:** Rebel assistance

### SE8 Waiter Droid, page 78

**Height:** 1.77m (5ft 10in)

**Function:** Serving guests

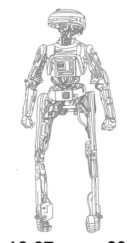

### L3-37, page 80

**Height:** 1.79m (5ft 10in)

**Function:** Piloting the *Millennium Falcon*

## Professor Huyang, page 82

**Height:** 1.8m (5ft 11in)
**Function:** Teaching young Jedi

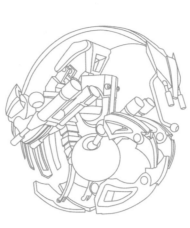

## Droideka, page 84

**Height:** 1.83m (6ft)
**Function:** Rolling into battle

## Police Droid, page 86

**Height:** 1.83m (6ft)
**Function:** Protecting Coruscant

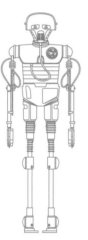

## 2-1B, page 88

**Height:** 1.85m (6ft 1in)
**Function:** Medical aid

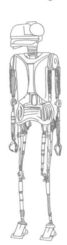

## EV-9D9, page 90

**Height:** 1.9m (6ft 2in)
**Function:** Overseeing droids
in Jabba's Palace

## Battle Droid, page 92

**Height:** 1.91m (6ft 3in)
**Function:** Simple battle soldiers

## Commando Droid, page 94

**Height:** 1.91m (6ft 3in)
**Function:** Battle soldiers

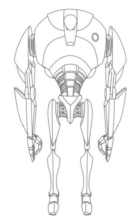

## Super Battle Droid, page 96

**Height:** 1.91m (6ft 3in)
**Function:** Advanced battle soldiers

## IG-88, page 98

**Height:** 1.93m (6ft 4in)
**Function:** Bounty hunter

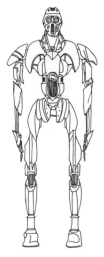

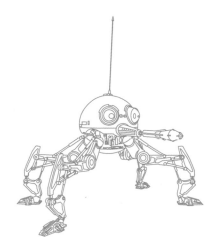

**R1-G4, page 100**
Height: 1.94m (6ft 4in)
Function: Piloting assistance

**MagnaGuard, page 102**
Height: 1.95m (6ft 5in)
Function: Bodyguard

**Dwarf Spider Droid, page 104**
Height: 1.98m (6ft 6in)
Function: Battling in narrow spaces

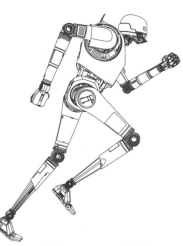

**Peazy, page 106**
Height: 2.06m (6ft 9in)
Function: Communications assistance
for the Resistance

**K-2SO, page 108**
Height: 2.2m (7ft 3in)
Function: Spying against
the Empire

**CC-4M, page 110**
Height: 2.67m (8ft 9in)
Function: Heavy lifting

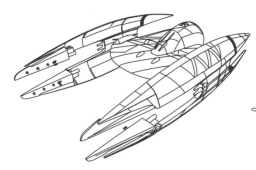

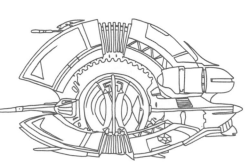

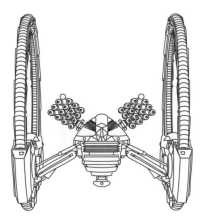

**Vulture Droid, page 112**
Length: 3.5m (11ft 6in)
Function: Battles in space

**Droid Tri-Fighter, page 114**
Length: 5.4m (17ft 8in)
Function: Battles in space

**Hailfire Droid, page 116**
Height: 6.8m (22ft 4in)
Function: Battle tank